Table of Contents

How to Play Craps

A Beginner to Expert Guide to Get You from the Sidelines to Running the Craps Table

HOW TO PLAY CRAPS

a beginner to expert guide

Steven Hartman

Table of Contents

Chapter 1Chapter 1
Welcome to the Craps Table!

You've heard the sudden bursts of cheers as you've strolled past the crowded Craps table.

You have even seen the countless TV shows and movies with the dice flying in slow motion over the green felt before knocking against the wall. The dealer barks out, "Winner!" and then the table roars with applause.

Now you want in.

But as you step up to an empty, unused craps table in a Vegas casino just to survey the complex boxes with terms like "Field" and "Pass Line", you're hesitant. You have second thoughts about going to an active table and putting $20 down because it just seems so impossible to play.

And then there isn't just one dealer like at the blackjack table or roulette wheel, but four!

A bead of sweat tickles your brow and you walk away from the intimidating Craps table and decide to invest your money at the Wheel of Fortune slot machine or tackle a few hands at the three-card poker table.

Go Back!

This book is designed for the beginner who has always wanted to experience the thrill of throwing the dice but was too afraid to learn how to play.

Worry not, shooter, this guide will have everything you need to step up to the table with confidence and have fun playing the wild game of Craps!

What This Book Will Teach You

The Absolute Basics

The first part of this book is going to explain the bare bones of Craps. This will be a short introduction into throwing the dice and what the numbers mean when they come up.

The Table

The second part of this book will explain the Craps table and break down what the numbers and terms on the green felt means.

Playing the Game

We will then explain the game in further detail and what to expect when the dice goes out, when you can bet, when you may win or lose money, and when your bet is safe.

Beyond the Basics

Now that you know the table and the basics, it's time to go beyond the basics. What are some fun bets to play? Why are some people making strange bets?

Fun Lingo!

Part of the fun of playing Craps is the seemingly goofy lingo that goes along with it. "Yo, 11," "Nina at the Marina," and "Crap check," are just a few examples of what you can shout out or what the dealers may call out.

Never, Ever!

After you spend a few minutes at the Craps table, you will discover that there is a lot of superstition. This means certain words or phrases uttered will give you death stares and looks of concern. We will cover the words you should avoid when at the table and proper etiquette.

Your First Time

Finally, we will give you a few tips on what you should do when you step up to the table for the first time.

Quick Story

A few months after I turned 21, my uncle insisted that I learned how to play Craps. We headed out to a nearby casino where he spent 5-10 minutes explaining the process and giving me a lesson on the game.

At the end of his lecture, he said, "Okay, let's go have lunch and then come back and play. Once you have money down, you'll learn real quick how it all works."

That stuck with me because I fully believe it. There is nothing like getting your hands dirty when it comes to learning. You could read all the material you want on how to drive a car but until you put the car into D and step on the gas pedal, you won't completely grasp the concept.

This book is going to teach you how to play Craps, but you will really learn how the game goes once you have money on the table.

Chapter 2
The Absolute Basics

This will by no means cover the game of Craps, but this section is going to briefly tell you how the game is played. This will make learning everything else a little easier.

Craps is played with a pair of 6-sided dice.

The first roll of the dice is called the come out roll.

- If the shooter rolls a 7 or 11, it's a winner.

- If the shooter rolls a 2, 3, or 12, it's called Craps and it loses.

- If the shooter rolls a 4, 5, 6, 8, 9, or 10, that number becomes the point. You then win by rolling the point before rolling a 7. It doesn't matter how many times you roll; the table does not lose unless the shooter rolls 7. (There are other ways to win, but more on that later)

- If the shooter makes the point, the game essentially restarts. They keep the dice and come out again.

And that really is the absolute basics of the game.

Chapter 3

The Green Felt

All the numbers and boxes can be somewhat overwhelming but we're going to break it down so that you have an easier time comprehending what it all means.

This is where playing Craps gets a little tricky because it's hard to explain the table without also explaining how the game is played. You know the basics from the previous chapter so that should help out. We will pepper this chapter with a little more about the game but won't go into much detail.

Picture yourself at the far end of one side of the table.

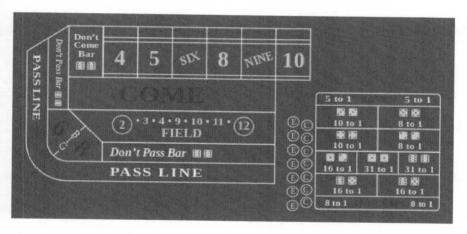

The Pass Line

The Pass Line means you are playing based on the roller. Once you place a chip down into this area, you cannot remove it until you win…that is unless you lose, then the dealer will take it down for you.

Don't Pass Bar

Placing a chip in the Don't Pass Bar section means you are betting against the roller – essentially, you are playing with the casino because if the roller loses, you win.

Big 6 and Big 8

The Big 6 and Big 8 on the corner pay even money. You can place a chip down at any time and remove it at any time (so long as you haven't lost it). Don't place or remove a bet if the dice are out. You have the power to put down and pick up your own chip, you do not need the dealer to do it for you.

Field

There are 7 numbers in the section known as the field: 2, 3, 4, 9, 10, 11, and 12. The field is a one-time bet which means you win or lose your money based on the next roll after you put the money down. Casinos have different payouts for this section but you will receive even money ($5 bet pays $5) unless it is a 2 or 12 which generally will pay 2:1 or 3:1 odds on your money. A $5 bet in the field on a 2 or 12 roll can win you $10 or $15.

Very rarely will the remaining numbers of 3, 4, 9, 10, and 11 pay greater than even money; the exception being that 3 or 11 may have higher odds.

Come and Don't Come Bar

When a roller is shooting for the first time, it's called a come out roll. The areas labeled Come and Don't Come Bar are designed for those wanting to place a bet similar to a come out roll after the shooter has started rolling the dice and a number (or point) has already been established.

Now, you may already be confused, but don't worry, this will make sense when we get into the way the game is played.

Points

Points are those six numbers up top: 4, 5, 6, 8, 9, and 10. Without getting into too much detail yet, the points are determined when the roller shoots. If they roll one of those six numbers, in order for you to win, they need to reroll that number before rolling a 7 (more on this later).

The Middle of the Table

As you can see there are pictures of dice, numbers, and odds. The odds may vary based on the casino but these are generally what you can expect.

- One-Time Bets

  - Seven – This is a one-time bet when you think the roller is about to roll a 7. It generally pays 5:1.

  - Any Craps – This one-time bet means you are betting on the roller shooting a 2, 3, or 12 on the next roll.

  - 2, 3, 11, 12 – These are listed as dice just above the "Any Craps" box. These are also one-time bets with varying odds of winning. The difference between these numbers and the "Any Craps" section is that you are betting on the individual number and not the 4 numbers as a whole – that's why the odds of winning are lower.

- The Hard Ways

  - The hard ways are the dice with 2 x 2s, 2 x 3s, 2 x 4s, 2 x 5s, respectively. When you bet a hard way, you're gambling that the roller will roll two dice with the same amount of dots (2 x 1s and 2 x 6s are not included here because that's the only way a 2 or 12 can come up).

  - An example is in order to roll 8, you can roll these combinations: 2 & 6, 3 & 5, or 4 & 4. If you roll a 2 & 6 or 3 & 5, it's called an easy eight. If you roll a 4 & 4, it's called a hard eight.

  - When you place a bet on a hard eight, for example, you are betting that IF the shooter rolls an 8, it will be 4 & 4. If they roll it any other way, you lose.

C / E

Next to the middle boxes are circles with a C or an E. The C stands for Craps and the E stands for 11. These are one time bets as well so betting here means you are anticipating that the next roll will be an 11 to win E or a 2, 3, or 12 to win C.

This is a lot to digest. The good news is that, as a beginner, you probably won't even need to know what half this stuff is anyway. You're going to start off dipping your toe in the shallow end and slowly work your way in. Over time, you will understand much more and increase your level of fun; and hopefully your chip count.

Now, let's learn how to play craps!

Chapter 4
Playing the Game

Take a deep breath, pull some money out of your pocket, and get ready to play some Craps.

For the sake of learning, we will assume you are playing at a $10 minimum table and that you are playing with $10 for each bet unless the type of bet allows for a $1 bet.

We will also assume that you are the one with the dice.

If you approach with cash, always wait until after the current roller shoots, then you can place your money on the table to be turned into chips.

Once you receive your chips, place a $10 chip on the Pass Line in front of you.

The Stick Man (the person with the stick) will usually give you 5 dice to choose from – remember this is a superstitious game and people like choices. Grab two dice and wait for the Stick Man to remove the remaining three.

The dealers may bark out, "Dice are out!", "Shooter out!", "No more bets!", or they may simply wait in silence for you to throw.

Recapping the Absolute Basics?

The first roll is called the come out roll

- If you roll a 7 or 11, you automatically win. The $10 on the Pass Line gets you an additional $10 as well as the other players betting the Pass Line.

  - Rolling a 7 or 11 on the come out roll is sure to get some cheers. Feel free to cheer as well - you're making people money and you get to roll again.

- If you roll a 2, 3, or 12, you automatically lose. The dealers take the $10 and, in order to keep playing, you need to put another $10 on the Pass Line.

  - You still have the dice and get to roll again if you put another $10 down.

  - The 2, 3, and 12 are considered "Craps".

- If you roll a 4, 5, 6, 8, 9, or 10, the point has been established and you keep playing.

What's a Point?

- A point or number is 4, 5, 6, 8, 9, or 10.

- The dealers will place an ON button on the point so the table knows what number needs to be rolled in order to win.

How Do I Win Once a Point Has Been Established?

For example, if you roll a 6 on your come out roll, the point is 6. You can roll any number and not lose with the exception of 7.

If you roll a 6, you win!

If you roll a 7 at any time after the point has been established, you lose.

After you make the point, the table basically resets (although you'll still see bets on the table — we'll get to that in a minute). This means you're coming out again and in order to win on the Pass Line, you have to roll a 7 or 11. If you roll a 4, 5, 6, 8, 9, or 10, that is the new point.

How Do I Lose Once a Point Has Been Established?

Roll a 7. That's it. As long as you don't roll a 7 after a point has been established, you can essentially roll forever until you roll the point.

Quick Story

I had taught many friends how to play Craps. One time in Las Vegas we were on the way to grab some breakfast when we saw an empty Craps table. "One quick round," one of my friends said and we all stepped up and put $5 down on the Pass Line (it was a $5 minimum table).

There were 4 of us: 3 guys and 1 lady. Again, this being a superstitious game we told the Stick Man to give the dice to Lady Luck. She picked her two dice and rolled…a 12. This being the come out roll, we all lost our money.

And that, my friends, was indeed a quick round of Craps.

Playing the Odds:

There are different odds when it comes to landing on any specific number because of the various ways the number can come up. The chances of rolling a 7 are far greater than rolling a 10, per se.

- You can land on 7 by rolling: 1 & 6, 2 & 5, 3 & 4, 4 & 3, 5 & 2, or 6 & 1.

- You can land on 10 by rolling: 4 & 6, 6 & 4, or 5 & 5.

- You can create a 7 by using any number on the dice but with 10, you can only use 4, 5, 6 to achieve 10.

- On any given roll, the chances of rolling a 7 are: 16.7%

- On any given roll, the chances of rolling a 10 are: 8.3%

When you're playing, you have money on the Pass Line but you can also place money behind your Pass Line bet. This is called playing the odds and they pay higher than even money.

If you put an additional $10 behind the Pass Line and the point is...

- 6 or 8, the odds are 6:5 meaning your $10 wins $12.

- 5 or 9, the odds are 3:2 meaning your $10 bet wins $15.

- 4 or 10, the odds are 2:1 meaning your $10 bet wins $20

  But if you roll a 7, you lose it all.

Note: DO NOT EVER put money in this area unless you intend on gambling it because the casino will consider it a bet, even if you don't. And, if the point loses, pleading ignorance is not a viable excuse – they will take it.

Playing the Numbers:

After rolling a few times and watching others throw money down, you may begin to feel more comfortable and want to get a little more adventurous. Most likely you rolled a 10 and seemed to roll every single number twenty times before hitting that 10 and you want to make more money just like the others seem to be doing.

"I see people betting on the numbers," you say to one of the Craps dealers. "How do I do that?"

Once a point has been established, you can put money down on any of the numbers up top.

When you place money on a number, all the roller has to do is roll that number for you to win. If they roll a 7, you lose it.

Each number has different odds which will determine the amount of money you can win.

- 6 or 8 pays $7 for every $6 you put down.

- 5 or 9 pays $7 for every $5 you put down.

- 4 or 10 pays $9 for every $5 you put down.

And when you win, you can keep your bet on the number. If you're feeling a little anxious, just tell the dealer you want to bring your money down and you get it back.

*Notice that placing a bet on a number and putting a bet "behind the Pass Line" pays different odds. When you put odds behind the line, the casino pays you true odds whereas placing a bet on a number pays a little less.

What happens if the point is 6, I put money on 8, and the dealer rolls a 6?

Good question!

Your money is perfectly safe when the dealer is coming out again. All the points are considered "Off".

And best of all, on the come out roll, if the shooter rolls a 7, your money will not be lost.

But, this also means if you have money on an 8 and the shooter rolls an 8 coming out, you don't win either. The number and your money are simply not in play.

Using the same example from above, if your money is on the 8 and the shooter rolls an 8 coming out, you have two options:

- Take your money back.

- Move it to another point.

The Field:

There are 7 numbers in the section known as the Field: 2, 3, 4, 9, 10, 11 and 12.

Because Craps is all about gut-feelings, some people may think one of the numbers listed on the Field is due to come up on the next roll and decide to put money down.

Other people love playing the Field consistently.

The Field is a one-time bet and can be played at any time, even on the come out roll.

The Field is also a favorite for beginners because it's easy to understand and people generally do okay – although, this is a casino so the odds are not in your favor.

Some experts will say this is the worst bet on the table – here's why:

Of the 36 combinations that can come up on any roll of the dice, the numbers in the Field consist of 16 combinations. But, the numbers most likely to come up are: 5, 6, 7, 8, and 9. Of those 5 numbers most likely to be rolled, only one (9) is in the Field.

Come:

That big section in the center is there for a reason although it's not used very frequently.

The Come box is basically a second Pass Line bet.

If you put $10 down in Come, that means that the next roll is treated like a come out roll for that bet.

If you roll a 7 or 11, you win even money on that bet. If you roll a 2, 3, or 12, you lose.

If you roll a 4, 5, 6, 8, 9, or 10, then that $10 bet placed on Come as the point.

All the same rules apply for that bet as if you are playing a second Pass Line which also means that the dice need to come up with your point for you to win.

This money is in play even if someone wins the table's point and is coming out again. A 7 may win on the Pass Line, but you will lose your money.

Scenario #1:

The point is 8.

You place $10 into the Come section.

The next roll is 6 – your point is 6.

The next roll is 8. The Pass Line wins – nothing happens to your 6 but it's still in play.

Now, the table is coming out again and the shooter rolls 7.

The table is happy but you lose your 6.

Scenario #2

The point is 9.

You place $10 into the Come section.

The next roll is 5 – your point for that bet is 5.

The next roll is 9. The Pass Line wins – nothing happens to your 5 but it's still in play.

Now, the table is coming out again and the shooter rolls 8.

The Pass Line point is 8.

The next roll is 4 – nothing happens.

The next roll is 5 – you win!

The Hard Ways

"8 hard!" Someone shouted and tossed a $1 chip into the center of the table.

A $1 bet at a $10 minimum table?

Yes!

Those bets in the middle of the table can generally be made for $1 (this may differ based on the casino).

Focusing on the hard ways though, these are not one-time bets. For the 4 even numbers that can be points (4, 6, 8, and 10), you can bet that IF they come up then both dice will be the same number.

- 2 & 2 = 4

- 3 & 3 = 6

- 4 & 4 = 8

- 5 &5 = 10

If they come up like the above list, you win that money.

If, for instance, an 8 is rolled as a 5 & 3, you lose.

And, of course, if the roll is the 7, you lose.

Let's say you have $1 on the hard 8 but the point is 6. You roll a 6 and it's time to come out once again.

The dealer will generally ask if you want your hard ways on or working. This means that they are subject to the dice during the come out roll. A 7 means you lose, an 8 as a 5 & 3 or 6 & 2 means you lose, but the 4 & 4 is a winner.

The thing is, the dealer may not always ask if you want your hard ways on which means they are working. They may also say, "Hard ways working unless called off".

Always yell out, "hard ways off," if you don't want them working on the come out roll.

You can also pull this bet back whenever you want to.

What's a 2-Way Hard (number)?

Have you heard someone yell this out? And then the dealers thank them?

What you are doing is "tipping" the dealers. In this case, you could throw down $1 for you and $1 for the dealers (or $10 for you and $1 for the dealers). If the hard way comes up, then they get the money.

There is plenty more to go but this will get you through the first few times you play Craps.

Chapter 5
Beyond the Basics

Hopefully, you have had a few turns at the Craps table, learned a few new bets, and you are now ready to go beyond the basics.

There are still plenty of sections where you can throw down the chips and make some money.

Let's take a deeper look at the Craps table.

C/E

Next to the middle section of the table are circles with either C or E in them.

- E is for 11

- C is for Craps

These are one-time bets often played when coming out.

To play, most will toss a 2 x $1 chips toward the center and call out "C and E".

You can play them individually, and many do.

Throw a $1 chip and yell "11" or "Dollar Yo!" and the Stick Man will move your $1 to the E.

Or toss the $1 chip toward the center and say "Crap check" if you think the next roll is going to be a 2, 3, or 12.

Many people will use the crap check almost as insurance against the come out roll. Remember, if you roll a 2, 3, or 12 when coming out, you lose your Pass Line bet.

- E, or a bet on 11 in the center, generally pays 16:1 or 15:1 depending on the casino.

- C, or any craps, pays 7:1 or 8:1 depending on the casino.

Craps Bets

In the center section, at the bottom, are dice revealing a combination of 2, 3, 11, and 12. These are one-time bets which count for the next roll.

This area is often ignored because of the minimal chances that these numbers will come up. As you can see, the odds are fairly high with a roll of 2 or 12 boasting odds of 31:1.

Seven

This is one way to receive dirty looks at the table. If a point has been established and you want to bet that 7 will be the next roll, you have that option.

Since the table is hoping this is not the case, you may here a few curses and prayers that you're wrong being muttered under the breath of other players.

Hop

If you want to get very specific, you can play the hop. Most Craps tables will not have this option visible on the actual felt of the table, but it is available.

A hop is a one-time bet on the exact roll of the dice and you can do this for as little as $1.

For instance, you don't hop 8…you hop 5 & 3. And, if you wanted to bet 8 will come up specifically on the next roll, you can hop 2 & 6, 3 & 5 and 4 & 4. This bet will cost $3 (assuming you bet $1 on each).

A hop will pay either 15:1 or 30:1 depending on the number.

Does this ever work?

Quick Story

It's a rare feat to pull off a successful hop but I have witnessed it a handful of times. The same uncle who taught me how to play Craps won a miraculous hop. We were playing Craps at one of the unique Craps tables out there. This table was known as "Crapless" Craps. In this particular case, if you rolled a 2, 3, 11, or 12 on the come out roll, you didn't lose (or if 11, win), that number became the point. My uncle rolled a 2 coming out. He was unfamiliar with hop bets but I had learned about them on one of my many trips to Las Vegas. I told him about hop bets as he rolled a few more times then, excited about the chance to make a quick $31, he tossed a $1 chip to the center and shouted, "Hop me on my aces!" Lo and behold, his next roll was a 2 and collected.

Buy

As a beginner, you will probably not even think of buying a bet but we want to explain to you what it means.

I'm going to use the number 4 and 10 as an example because they are the most bought numbers.

Casinos pay $9 for every $5 you put down on the 4 or the 10. There is an option called buying. When you buy a number, you receive true odds for that number. 9:5 is not the true odds for 4 or 10, the true odds are 2:1.

Here is what you need to know about buying a number:

- 4 and 10 are the best numbers to invest in when buying.

- Generally, the minimum to buy a bet is $20 (almost never under that).

- The house takes a 5% commission on buys

   - $20 buy bet on 4 or 10 wins $40 - $1 commission = $39

   - $20 place bet on 4 or 10 wins $36

The reason 4 and 10 are the best numbers to buy is because you get the greatest amount back for your investment.

Buy Bet True Odds (also, behind the Pass Line odds):

- 4 and 10 = 2:1

- 5 and 9 = 3:2

- 6 and 8 = 6:5

Don't Pass Bar & Don't Come Bar, or how to make enemies at the Craps table

When you play Don't Pass Bar or Don't Come Bar, you're playing with the casino and not against it. Because almost every player at the table is trying to win money, they see you as the enemy.

- Don't Pass Bar – This works just like playing the Pass Line including the ability to put odds down. The difference is that you are betting with the casino. On the come out roll:

  - If the shooter rolls a 7 or 11, you automatically lose.

  - If the shooter rolls a 2, 3, or 12, you automatically win.

  - If the shooter rolls a 4, 5, 6, 8, 9, or 10 then that still becomes the point, however, you are betting that the shooter rolls a 7 before the point. If they do, you win. If they roll the point, you lose.

- Don't Come Bar – This is similar to the Come section on the table but you are betting against it. You can bet Don't Come Bar once a point has been established on the table. And, just like placing a bet on Come:

  - If the shooter rolls a 7 or 11 on the next roll, you automatically lose.

  - If the shooter rolls a 2, 3, or 12 on the next roll, you automatically win.

— If the shooter rolls a 4, 5, 6, 8, 9, or 10 then that still becomes the point, however, you are betting that the shooter rolls a 7 before the point designated with the Don't Come Bar roll. If they do, you win. If they roll the point, you lose.

— With Don't Come Bar, let's say your point is 6 but the point on the table is 8. If the shooter rolls an 8 then you won't win or lose. It's almost like you are playing in a separate game when you bet Come or Don't Come Bar. Technically, if the shooter makes the table's point and then rolls a 7 on the come out roll, everyone, including you, would win.

Quick Story

My brother doesn't play Craps unless I'm around and he loves playing Don't Pass Bar. As a very logical thinker, he knows the odds of winning are better when placing that bet and I would suspect that his objective is 50% winning, 50% annoying me.

There are lots of ways to play the game of Craps and as you play more, you will be more interested in taking chances and trying new bets. Some you will never even think about doing and others will become your favorite.

Each time you play is different and, superstitious or not, there is a certain vibe that seems to be around a table when playing. If you feel that the table is cold, maybe hold off.

Quick Story

I taught a friend how to play Craps and one time on a trip to Vegas without me, he found his path to victory through the Field and made a considerable amount of money. His next trip was one with me and he wanted to make his next big money by playing the same way. Unfortunately, the dice were not rolling in his favor and he went through most of his money in a short amount of time. There is no one way to play the game of Craps.

Chapter 6

The Lingo

If there is one thing I have taken away from Craps, it's the fun phrases and the lingo that is heard around the table. Some dealers are extremely entertaining with what they come up with.

Here are some of the phrases you can use or may hear around the Craps table:

Dollar Yo! – This means you are putting $1 down on 11. You are betting that the next roll is going to be 11 and the Stick Man will often place it on the E.

Crap Check – When you want to bet that 2, 3, or 12 (Craps) will be the next roll. This is often done on the come out roll. The Stick Man will place your bet on the C.

C and E – When you call out "C and E" you are betting that the next roll will be 2, 3, 11, or 12. The Stick Man will place your bet on the C and E circles, respectively.

$5 Whirl or $5 World – This can be any amount, but a whirl bet is basically placing $1 on 2, 3, 7, 11, and 12. Instead of saying $1 for each, you can call out "Five Dollar World!"

Quick Story

$5 whirl bets can be fun to do especially on the come out roll because you make money if the 2, 3, 7, 11, or 12 hit. This is something I do occasionally and one time, it really paid off. I did $5 whirl then rolled one of the numbers in the series probably 5 or 6 times in a row, in some cases, it was 12 which paid 31:1. I had made well over $100 before the point was even established. I have yet to experience this magic a second time.

Pressure or Press – Let's say you are playing the numbers and you bet $10 on 9. Then you roll a 9. You will win $18 (9 pays 9:5). If you tell the dealer to "press it" or "pressure", they will add $10 to your bet and give you back $8. Now you have a $20 bet on your 9.

Play the Outside – There are players who want to play a lot of points and try to make a lot of money doing it. They will put down money and say "Play the Outside". This means they are placing bets on the numbers: 4, 5, 9, and 10.

Play the Inside – When you play the inside, you are placing money down on the numbers: 5, 6, 8, and 9.

Hot Dice – The shooter is doing well and making the table money.

The Numbers

2

Aces or Snake Eyes – Rolling a 2 (1 & 1)

3

Acey-Deucy - Rolling a 3 (1 & 2)

4

Little Joe – Rolling a 4 (2 & 2). Also called a hard 4.

5

No Field 5 – The dealer will call this out if the shooter rolls a 5, probably because 5 and 9 sound alike.

Fever – Rolling a 5.

7

Big Red – Because of the superstition at Craps tables, you do not want to say the number 7 but if you do decide to bet on 7 after the point has been established, you can call out "Big Red" and the dealer should know you are betting that the next roll is going to be a 7.

Seven Out – This is when a 7 is rolled after the point has been established. The dealer will call "Seven Out".

8

Square Pair - Hard 8 (4 & 4)

The Ole Loop-Dee Loop – This is any 8.

9

Nina – If a dealer calls out "Nina from Pasadena" or a fellow shooter says "Come on, Nina!" then they are referring to 9.

Center Field – When a shooter rolls a 9 which is the median of all the numbers in the field. Dealers will often yell out "9! 9! Centerfield 9" when it comes up.

The Ole Iron Bucket – The first time I heard this, I needed an explanation but soon adopted this as one of my favorites. This is a dice roll of 4 & 5. Putting the two dice together slightly resembles an iron bucket...if you use your imagination. The four is the handle and the five is the bucket. Again, use your imagination.

10

General Patton – The roll is a Hard 10 (5 & 5). This is a play on a 5-star general.

11

Yo or Yo-leven – This is the term for 11.

12

Boxcars or Midnight – Rolling a 12.

Hard 12 - Sometimes both dealers and players alike will make fun of the fact that you can only get a 12 by rolling 2 x 6's and call it a hard 12.

Now, some of these like "Crap Check" and "Dollar Yo" are well known and the dealer will know what you mean if you call it out. When it comes to numbers, say what you want. If you say, "$10 on the Iron Bucket," they may look at you strangely and want an explanation.

Chapter 7

Never, Ever!

There is a lot of action that can happen all at once at a Craps table and sometimes you don't realize you are doing something wrong. Here are a few things you will want to avoid so you're not upsetting the casino or your fellow players.

Saying Craps or 7

We have covered quite a few times how superstitious a table can be. Unless you want a lot of upset people, avoid saying Craps or 7. Considering that 7 is the most likely number to come up when rolling the dice, you won't want to be blamed for it if it does and people lose.

Quick Story

I was at a casino with a bunch of people for a pre-wedding party. A few of us were playing Craps when a member of the party, who knew almost nothing about the game and was probably a little drunk, stepped up and said, "How do you play again? Isn't craps a 7?" I do not believe he did this intentionally and he probably didn't know about the superstition. He did receive a lot of dirty looks when the next roll was a 7 and we lost money.

The Dice Are Out

If the shooter has been given the dice but has not thrown them yet, do not try to put money down. If the dice hit your hand and the roll is bad (they roll a 7 and lose or roll craps on the come out roll and lose) then they will blame you. The casino doesn't like this because they may see you as interfering.

The table is generally quiet before a roll because people are holding their breath waiting for a number, so if you say, "$10 in the field" or "hard eight" but don't actually put the money down (maybe you have it in your hand), more often than not, the dealer will hear you and acknowledge it.

Even if you lose, pay up. The dealer has the final say so if they don't hear you, then you will have to just deal with it – it's not worth holding up the table.

Don't Do Anything with The Dice Except Throw It

Ah yes, the dice are in your hand and you want to blow on them like they do in the movies. You may want your spouse, significant other or cute stranger to do it too. DON'T. Movies aren't real life and the casino does not want you to do this because people try to cheat sometimes. They want to have eyes on the dice at all times.

Keep the dice near or below the padded area along the Craps table, shake them a bit if you want, and then throw them.

Also, do not switch hands. If you pick up the dice with your right hand, that's the hand you throw with. Don't move them to your left hand as you shake them or anything like that. Again, the casino will not tell you more than once not to do it.

There is a lot of strange stuff people can do with dice before throwing it like putting them on a certain number or even tossing them high into the air. I would avoid this until you are more familiar with what you can and cannot do.

Don't Miss the Wall

This isn't so bad but this goes along with cheating. There are notions that the way dice are rolled, and not hitting any barriers, they can be manipulated into landing on a certain number. The casino will insist that you hit the wall. Missing it once every so often is no big deal, miss it a lot, and they may decide that you can't play anymore.

Don't Worry About Overthrowing

EVERYONE overthrows the dice. EVERYONE. Don't worry if you do it because it happens. Remember, the goal is to hit the back wall and sometimes dice slip when coming out of your hand – Hey, even the best pitchers throw a wild pitch every so often.

The roll won't count and you can choose a new dice.

The one you tossed halfway to the bar will be collected, the Box Man (the man in the center) will examine it and then it will go back with the dice not in use. All you have to do is choose another dice.

Superstitious? Let's say you have been really hot with a set of dice and you want that one back. Simply say so and 99.9% of the time they will accommodate you. The Box Man will examine it first and you will get it back.

But you should expect a little joking if you overthrow it. "Watch out, lady driver!" is often heard by one of the dealers if it's a woman who has overthrown it. Just take it in stride and have fun.

If You're Not Rolling, Don't Touch the Dice

Whether they knock down your chips or go deep into the corner where you may be situated, the Stick Man has a stick for a reason. Do not touch the dice.

There are two exceptions to this rule though:

- The dice go off the table and, as a courtesy, you go get it. Since they are going to inspect the dice anyway, this is okay. Just place it down on the felt and they will take care of it.

- The dice land where your chips are. Let's say a wild dice thrower lands a good shot off your chest and it falls on your line of chips. In this case, just pick up the dice and place it on the felt.

The overthrowing of the dice means the roll won't count so you won't be interfering.

No Dangling

There is a shelf under the Craps table where you can keep your drink and your cigarette. Don't hold either one over the table. The last thing you want to do is have ash from the cigarette spill to the green felt or the remainder of your beer cover the Pass Line.

Also, lots of people lean forward around the table. Avoid letting your hands drape down.

Even if you make any of these errors, I am confident the world is not going to end. I'm also sure you won't get kicked out of the casino; unless you keep it up. Just remember to pay attention of what's going on and keep clear of the dice if you aren't rolling.

And, if you really are nervous about rolling the dice, you have the option to pass it unless you are the only one at the table. People do this frequently for many reasons. Sometimes they just don't like rolling the dice or they are nervous. Some don't want to think that they could lose someone considerable amounts of money.

I would highly recommend rolling the dice though. It's a great experience, especially when you get on a hot streak.

Chapter 8
Come 7, Come 11

Here are a few tips on what you should do when you step up to the table for the first time.

If you want a warm welcoming, let the table know you're a first-time roller. You will probably get more cheers and encouragement.

I think we may have mentioned it once or twice but this is a game filled with superstition and no one gets people in the mood to cheer than the idea of "Beginner's Luck". Dealers are mostly more than willing to help out and offer suggestions. It also gives you some wiggle room in the event you do something you should never do like pass dice from one hand to the other.

Going to an emptier table at the beginning of your Craps journey allows you to see more of the action without being pressed in like a sardine at the busy tables.

As a beginner, there is nothing wrong with putting the minimum down on the Pass Line and just seeing what happens.

Are you ready to have some fun at the Craps table?

"New shooter coming out!"

Poker: How to Play Texas Hold'em Poker

A Beginner's Guide to Learn How to Play Poker, the Rules, Hands, Table, & Chips

POKER

HOW TO PLAY TEXAS HOLD'EM POKER

A Beginner's Guide to Learn How to
Play Poker, the Rules, Hands,
Table, & Chips

STEVEN HARTMAN

Table of Contents

Chapter 1
Welcome to the Poker Table!

From the celebrity tournaments on cable TV to the games played at home nationwide, poker can be filled with fun and suspense.

There are many versions of poker being played. Just in a casino, you can encounter:

- Poker Machines – Variations include five-card draw, Joker Poker, Deuces Wild, and dozens of others.

- Three Card Poker – A popular version played as part of the table games, this version combines the excitement of poker with the speed of table gaming.

- Pai Gow Poker – This table game can be awfully confusing at first to learn, but the dealers and players are generally very helpful. It is an exciting game often with lively conversation.

- Texas Hold 'Em – Recently becoming one of the most popular games in the casino, unlike other casino games, this one focuses on the players gambling against one another; not just against the dealer.

Texas Hold 'Em has similar rules to regular poker or five card draw, but the cards are dealt differently, and there are more opportunities to bet.

There is a diverse atmosphere to the Texas Hold 'Em tables, and no two will be alike (unlike Blackjack where everyone wants a

Blackjack or, at a minimum, for the dealer to bust). Some poker players play as seriously as if it were the World Series of Poker while others pop in out of curiosity and try their luck at a few hands.

Casino Texas Hold 'Em is a different ballgame than a Saturday night poker tourney with pizza and drinks. I'm not saying it isn't fun or that people don't chat and have a good time, but just like the serious gambler at any table in the casino, there are players who have zero interest in talking and play with a straight poker face the whole time. So, being one of the only games in a casino that pit players against players, and since there can only be one winner per hand, the spirit of competition is alive and well.

Who Benefits From This Book?

This book is designed for the beginner who has always wanted to sit at the oval Texas Hold 'Em table at a casino and understand the concept of the game but was too timid to try or wasn't sure how to play poker.

Whether you want to dip your toe in and see what the excitement is all about, or you want to jump all the way in and make the poker room a regular stop at the casino, this book will give you the basics of how to play poker.

What This Book Will Teach You

The Absolute Basics

The first part of this book is going to explain the very basics of poker, and it will give you the foundation of almost every other kind of poker out there.

You will also be introduced to what exactly this Texas Hold 'Em game is.

The Table

The second part of this book will explain the Texas Hold 'Em table. This portion will also give you the basic lingo, so you know what the big blind, small blind, and the dealer buttons mean.

Playing the Game

We will then explain the game in further detail and what to expect when the cards are dealt, when you can bet, raise, fold or go all in.

Advice on Becoming Good, or Not Losing as Much

By this point, you will know the table and how the game is played. Since you are new to it, there is some advice that will help you play a little more conservatively and combat the pitfalls that many Texas Hold 'Em players fall into, even the experienced ones.

Never, Ever!

Just like any other casino game, there is plenty of superstition. We will also cover what you should never do while sitting at the table as well as basic etiquette.

Witness the Impossible!

I want to utilize this chapter to tell one of the most incredible hands of poker I had ever seen while playing Texas Hold 'Em, which also highlights how the community cards, betting, and excitement of the game work.

There are a few lessons worth learning at the conclusion of the story.

Your First Time

Finally, we will give you a few tips on what you should do when you step up to the table for the first time. It may be very intimidating especially if the table is filled with very quiet, very serious players, but don't worry. Give it a chance and do your best.

We will also cover general tips to helping you make your first few trips to the table more enjoyable, and successful.

How Did Texas Hold 'Em Become SO Popular?

You would be hard-pressed to find an old western movie where a handful of gunslingers are situated around a round table sipping whiskey and playing Texas Hold 'Em. They played five-card draw – basically, you deal, you bet, winner takes the pot. Repeat. Then someone gets accused of cheating, and a shoot-out takes place.

There have been various versions of poker for nearly 200 years from five or seven card stud to Omaha High-Low. Texas Hold 'Em has origins dating back to the early 1900s.

So, how did Texas Hold 'Em become so popular, so fast?

It started in 2003 when a nobody in the world of poker entered an online poker tournament that gave him a seat at the World Series of Poker, and he won it all. Chris Moneymaker (the name only added to the sensationalism) planted the seed that literally anyone could win at poker at the highest level. Imagine a random fan getting pulled out of the stands in the middle of the MLB World Series and going on to hitting the game-winning home run!

But the rise in its immense popularity has one simple reason: Hockey.

Or lack thereof.

It was a matter of filling in empty time slots when sports networks could not air hockey games due to the 2004-2005 NHL lockout. Texas Hold 'Em was merely filler until the strike ended and hockey would be played once again.

Except, Texas Hold 'Em captured the attention of Americans and Canadians. People loved watching these eccentric players stand up, and pace during the Showdown and the commentators anticipate the odds of a player winning. Celebrity poker tournaments also started to air, and you could watch people like Paul Rudd, Sarah Silverman, Neil Patrick Harris and Ben Affleck play the game.

The rest is history.

Chapter 2
The Absolute Basics

Poker is played with a standard 52-card deck with Ace being the highest card and 2 being the lowest. The goal is to have the highest hand in a standard poker hierarchy which wins the pot. Within the hierarchy of hands, any number of variations can lead to a winning hand; against the other player that is.

Poker Hierarchy (from lowest to highest, including probabilities of getting this hand in Texas Hold 'Em):

- High Card – The lowest of the lows in the poker hierarchy, it basically means your hand is nothing more than a set of random cards with the highest card in your hand being your best variation.

- There is a 100% guarantee that you will always have a high card.

- One Pair – You have two cards of the same number within your hand. Ex: 2 x 6's

- Approximately 82% chance of getting a pair.

- Two Pair – You have two sets of pairs. Ex: 2 x 6's and 2 x K's.

- This is where odds drop dramatically in the poker hierarchy. The chances of getting two pair are approximately 39%.

- Three of a Kind – This means you have three cards of matching numbers amongst your set. Ex: 3 x 8's.

- Odds are 15% of getting a Three of a Kind.

- Straight — A straight is a variation of five consecutive cards. Ex: 8, 9, 10, J, Q or 3, 4, 5, 6, 7. The suits do not have to match.

- Odds of getting a straight are 10%.

- Flush — A flush means you have five cards of a similar suit. They do not have to be in any consecutive order. Ex: 5 x Spades

- The probability of getting a flush is 5.8%.

- Full House — A full house is a combination of a two pair and a three pair in the same five card hand. Ex: 2 x Aces + 3 x 8's.

- Although not impossible, the probability of getting a full house is 2.8%.

- Four of a Kind — You have all four suits of a single number. Ex: 4 x 10's.

- In Texas Hold 'Em, the probability of getting a four of a kind drops below 1% down to 0.2%.

- Straight Flush — A very rare occurrence, the straight flush is a series of consecutive numbers all of the same suit. Ex: 4, 5, 6, 7, 8 all of which are hearts.

- Near impossible, the probability of getting a straight flush is 0.03%

- Royal Flush – The hardest hand to get in poker, a royal flush is a 10, J, Q, K, A all the same suit.

- There are only 4 ways to get a royal flush making it the most difficult. The probability of getting a royal flush is 0.003%.

The probability of these hands showing up in Texas Hold 'Em is far greater than in a standard five-card draw because you are collectively playing with 7 cards, as opposed to 5.

Five Card Draw vs. Texas Hold 'Em

Five card draw consists of five cards being dealt to each player face down. Unless it is by accident, these cards are only seen by the respective player. After looking at the hands, the players can replace however many cards they do not want in an attempt to achieve a higher hand. After all the players are dealt their new cards, they are revealed, and the winner is announced.

Of course, there is betting that goes on, but I wanted to explain poker in its simplest form.

For Texas Hold 'Em, there are two cards dealt face down to each player – called hole cards or pocket cards.

Someone who was dealt a pair refers to their cards collectively as "pocket (number)." Dealt two Aces? You have pocket Aces.

After viewing these cards, the first three of five additional cards are dealt face up into the center of the table. These are considered community cards and anyone at the table is able to use them to fulfill their hand.

This means that if there is a King available and you need it to complete a three of a kind, you can. But someone else can use the King for their straight. Both of you can use it – but they would win.

As this is gambling, these series of cards being dealt are given fun names:

- The Flop – these are the first three additional cards

- The Turn – the fourth card

- The River – the fifth card

Just like five card poker, there is gambling which takes place throughout the various dealings.

If are familiar with any version of poker, you will find it easier to get acquainted with Texas Hold 'Em.

Now that you know the absolute basics of the game, it is time to head to the table.

Chapter 3
The Table

While Vegas is known for their flashy tables, side bets and cramped seating at full tables, the Texas Hold 'Em tables are slightly different. In fact, if you go to a casino, Texas Hold 'Em is often played in a separate room from the main casino or behind a barrier.

In the beginning, to accommodate the popularity, casinos would put up rope barriers and create makeshift rooms in the casino.

Depending on how busy the room is, you may not actually be able to sit down and play right away but rather put your name in as if you were waiting for a table at a restaurant on a Saturday night.

The table itself is far from flashy. A lot of green felt, generally ten seats for players and one for the dealer. There may be markings in the center where the dealer places the Flop, the Turn and the River but there really isn't much to a table.

In regards to the dealer, there is not one spot better than the other – just like Craps. The dealer is simply there to deal the cards and control the money.

Unlike Blackjack where the first and last players around the table can sway the cards dealt around the table as well as the dealer's final card, the dealer is not involved in the play itself. They are just the one to shuffle and deal the cards, dole out the winnings, and pocket what belongs to the casino.

There are generally three buttons on the table as well. They are markers to indicate the player who is considered the dealer followed by the small blind and then the big blind.

The dealer/player acts as if they are the ones dealing the cards, which means the person to their immediate left is the first person to receive the first card in the deal.

The two blind buttons force at least two players to put money in the pot. The person immediate to the left of the dealer/player has the small blind button, and the person to their left gets the big blind button.

More about the blinds later though.

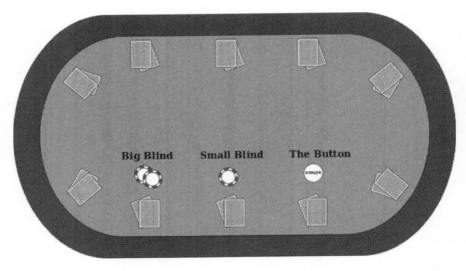

(I do not have the rights to this picture)

Now you know the basics of poker and the Texas Hold 'Em table, it is time to learn how to play the game.

Chapter 4
Playing the Game

We have touched on the basics of Texas Hold 'Em when explaining the differences between this version of poker and five card draw.

Let's dive a little deeper into the game.

When you sit down at the table, the dealer generally will not turn your cash into chips until it is between hands; there are some cases that you will get your chips prior to sitting down.

Each player is dealt two cards, face down.

The Buttons:

As noted in the previous chapter, there are 3 buttons that are on the table. If you have the dealer button, you are considered the "dealer" which means the cards are dealt by the actual dealer from your perspective.

The two blind buttons, small blind, and big blind, indicate the two players who must put money into the pot in order to play.

Let's say you are sitting at a table with a $10 minimum bet, the big blind must ante $10 whereas the small blind antes $5.

The player clockwise to the big blind can choose whether to bet the minimum or fold based on their two cards. They can bet however much they want (unless you are sitting at a limit table in which there is a maximum they can bet at one time) and the process continues clockwise until reaching the small blind.

Hypothetically, let's say every player at the table chose to put in $10, the small blind must equal the $10 (remember, they only had to put $5 in at the beginning) to continue playing. If they choose to fold their cards, they forfeit their $5 ante.

In this same hypothetical, the big blind can simply choose to check and continue playing without having to put more money into the pot.

If you are the big blind and no one else has raised the bet, you should not fold your calls – you are already invested and have nothing to lose by continuing.

Betting

After you received your cards and the first round of betting has taken place, the dealer then places three cards into the center of the table – The Flop.

This is where things start to get a little more interesting. Each player has five cards to work with; three of which belong to the community.

Unlike the previous round when the big blind and the small blind had to ante up in order to play, they no longer are required to make a bet.

The player clockwise to the dealer (the small blind, unless they folded), gets to bet first. They have the option of checking if they decide not to bet at this moment or bet however they choose, respective of limits.

Continuing clockwise, the players can bet how they see fit. However, at limit tables, they are set to specific amounts. For instance, if you are seated at that $10 table, you would bet $10. The person to your left can then see your $10 and raise you $10.

This type of playing gets rid of the person who sits at a $10 table, sees your $10 and then raises $1,000.

The betting continues until the player who needs to contribute the most calls or folds, as oppose to raise again.

Let's put this into action:

There is you and 5 other players at the table.

You: Bet $10

Player #1: Sees your $10

Player #2: Folds

Player #3: Sees your $10

Player #4: Folds

Player #5: Sees your $10 and raises $10.

You: See Player #5's $10 (so now you have $20 invested in the game)

Player #1: Folds

Effectively, there are two players going forward. Once a player folds, they lose whatever they have bet thus far including Player # 1 who saw your $10 bet.

Now, if you have a good hand, you could have seen Player #5's $10 and raise another $10.

Essentially, every player could check, and therefore no bets are placed in the round. This is what differentiates betting after the Flop versus betting with the big and small blinds. That first round could very well play out the same way with the exception that two players are forced to start the betting.

The next round of betting comes after the Turn (the fourth community card), and a final round of betting comes after the River (the final of five community cards).

The dealer will usually burn a card before revealing the Turn card and again before dealing the River – this means they take the next card in their card and remove it from play.

Determining the Winner

Hold on tight because this is where things can get a little confusing. How can a winning hand be confusing?

It is not so much about determining the winner as it is determining what the winning hand is. Although there are 7 cards in play (your two and the five in the middle), the winning hand are the five best cards that make that winning hand.

Sometimes it is easy to determine, other times, not so much.

For the purposes of explanation, we will act as if there are two remaining players: you and one other player. We also will not talk strategy here.

Finally, unless indicated, no hand provides a flush (5 cards of the same suit).

Scenario #1:

Your Cards: A, A

Player's Cards: 10, 9

5 Cards: A, K, J, 2, 7

Remember, we must look at the winning hand. In this case, it is a three of a kind (3 x Aces). You would win the pot.

Scenario #2:

Your Cards: 3, 5

Player's Card: 7, 8

5 Cards: 4, 6, 2, 9, 5

In this scenario, both players' hands are a straight. However, you would lose because, numerically, your straight is not as high.

Your Hand = 2-3-4-5-6

Player's Hand = 5, 6, 7, 8, 9

Are you crazy for staying and playing? Well, it is kind of crazy to continue with a 3 and a 5 in the hole, but you did get a straight in the flop. They just got a better straight later on.

Scenario #3

Your Cards: A, K

Player's Cards: A, J

5 Cards: 2, 4, A, A, 10

Take a minute, look at your hand, the other player's hand and the five cards in the middle. What do you think is the winning hand, not the winning player?

If you guessed correctly, the winning hand is A, A, A, K, 10. And, congratulations. You won!

Wait…if you are going with the 5 best cards to create a winning hand, wouldn't it be A, A, A, K, J?

Good point. But the winning hand is the 5 best cards out of 7, not picking from other hands. Here are all the cards that each player could use to create a winning hand.

Your Cards: A & K (hole cards), 2, 4, A, A, 10

Player's Cards Cards: A & J (hole cards), 2, 4, A, A, 10

Your three Aces followed by a King and 10, beat his three aces followed by a J and 10 because the King is higher than the Jack.

Scenario #4:

Your Cards: A, A

Player's Cards: K, K

5 Cards: 6, 7, 8, 9, 10

So, who wins the pot?

Remember, the winning hand, the best five card hand, is the one that matters. In this case, the winning hand is the straight.

When the best hand is found in the five cards in the center or if the final players have the equivalent of the same hand, the pot is split.

In this case, the pot is split between you and the other player.

The Showdown

The Showdown is when the final players are set to reveal their cards. Who goes first?

The last person to raise will be the one who is called upon to reveal their hand. If you made the final raise and the other players call, it is up to you to show your hand.

If everyone checks after the River, the person to the left of the dealer will be the first player to reveal their winning hand.

Let's say you were bluffing the whole time or you simply see the other players' hands, and you know you lost, you actually do not have to show your hole cards. Keeping them face down, you can simply put them down.

Other players can do this to. The only players who actually have to show their hands are the first person who reveals their cards (per the above), and the player that won. If you see that you did not win and you were not forced to show your hand, it is recommended to never reveal what you had.

Now that you know about the game and how it is played, let's move on to some advice on how to become a better player.

Chapter 5
Advice on Becoming Good, or Not Losing as Much

How do you become a good player? There are generally two things that help a player become good:

- Understanding probabilities

- Reading people

You can see the probabilities of being dealt a certain hand and creating a five card combination of various ranks at the beginning of the book. While you do not have to memorize these probabilities, you can recognize the likelihood of getting a full house versus a three of a kind is significantly more difficult. But you should also recognize that the chance of getting that three of a kind is still a low 15%.

In regards to reading people, there is plenty of advice to share, but it is all meaningless unless you know who you are dealing with. Someone sweating may be working on a bluff, or it may be warm. Suddenly sitting up straighter might indicate two good hole cards, or they are uncomfortable.

So, how do you read people?

Observation.

Betting patterns are key. Do they fold a lot or not really bet? What if they suddenly started betting aggressively? That is a good indicator they are confident in their cards.

If you are good at reading people, you will be able to spot the differences in people's manners as the hands take place.

You have tells too. Make sure you know your behavior, and that will help you be a better player too.

How Not to Lose (too much) Money

Gambling is a risk, and there is no guarantee you will walk away with anything, unless you decide to walk away before you lose it all. So, while I cannot promise you will win all the time, here are some strategies and advice on how to minimize losing it all quickly.

First off:

Do not bet more than you can afford. This is a standard piece of advice when it comes to gambling, and it's true. While chasing the high that comes with a win, it is worth paying the mortgage rather than losing it in a game of cards.

Do Not...

- ...think you have to play every hand – While it is enticing to play in every round along with the experience of FOMO (Fear or Missing Out), if you want to take a break because the cards are not going your way, feel free to do so. Unless you are a dealer, big blind or small blind, there is no reason why you cannot sit out a round or two. Most casinos allow it. If you feel pressure from the table, you are allowed to get up and use the restroom – just leave your chips at the table to mark your spot and intention of returning. The dealer will accommodate.

- ...play every hand to see the Flop. While it is tempting, very tempting, to play along to see if you can get a good thing going in the Flop, it is an amateur move. Remember, playing to see the Flop is not free – it will cost you, at a minimum, the big blind. Now, if you are the big blind, then you should obviously not fold unless another player raises as the betting continues around the table. If that happens but you do not have the quality cards to risk going forward, sometimes it is worth forfeiting your blind.

- ...play with players that are significantly better than you. This may be hard to tell right from the start, but if you think everyone is a seasoned player, they are more than happy to take your money. Playing with better players, like anything else in life, is a great way to improve your own skill, but you have to be learning from them and not getting cleaned out. It's the difference between a high school Freshman playing against a Senior versus the same Freshman playing against Lebron James. One case you can learn from someone a little better, the other you are getting overpowered.

- ...forget to study other people. Some have a great poker face, and it is hard to figure out what they are thinking or intend on doing. By actively studying others though, you are learning the tricks and seeing when players tend to bluff, how they bet and how their emotions may change depending on their hand.

- ...show your cards. Really, if you don't have to, don't do it. There is nothing to be gained by showing another player your losing hand. It only gives them more information on how you play. Maybe you bluffed your way to the end, or maybe you played a little more aggressively with three of a kind...who cares? Unless you are forced to show your cards, keep them face down.

- ...think you are going to win. Yes, you would like to win. That is the point. But do not play every hand thinking it will be a winning hand. Sure, you have a straight, but it does not mean another player is not able to beat you. Even the hands of least probability and considered surefire wins can lose (as you will discover in chapter 7).

Playing at a table you can afford to play is crucial, especially for a beginner. Once you sit down, I recommend thinking of your stack of chips as if they were simply chips and not money.

Why is that?

When you play based on single chips and not money, you can play more efficiently. If there are 100 chips in the pot and there a few players left standing and to keep going is 1 more chip, then it is worth continuing. It is 1 chip for the chance to win 100 of them. Your 1% addition to the pot is worth the opportunity to win it.

On the other hand, if it is between you and a single player, they raise two chips against the six in the pile after the River, and you are bluffing, well, is it worth going forward?

It is up to each individual player to figure out where the point is that it is no longer worth risking more money. You should figure it out because when faced in that situation, many people tend to look back and see how many chips they have invested instead of deciding to cut their losses before they risk more.

Forget Your Emotions and Your Feelings

Simply put, poker is a game of probabilities. It is all math.

If you let your emotions get the best of you and you think the next one is the lucky one or that you have a feeling the 7 you need to complete the straight is coming up in the Turn then you are not playing the most intelligent way.

There is a lot of advice above and some that is missing, everyone will learn a lot of unintended lessons along the way. Regardless, this should help you gamble more responsibly and make the most out of your Texas Hold 'Em learning experience.

Now, let's discuss what you should never, ever do at the poker table.

Chapter 6
Never, Ever!

Feeling out a table and the personality of the people is often easy. There are chatty folks and silent poker players. You will be able to tell who is who and you have every right to keep your mouth shut or join in the conversation.

Poker is a social game, and you will find a lot of discussion going on about almost any topic - learning about where someone is from, what they do, or even what movies they recently saw are all good.

But there are some things you should never do at a poker table. Here is a head's up on what should be avoided.

Conversations

What's That?

Just like any table in Vegas or casino you step foot into, there is a lot of superstition involved in gambling. While those at the Craps table fear someone saying "7" and Blackjack players may knock the table in hopes of getting a 21, poker has the same superstitious people of their own.

Perhaps the biggest difference though is how customized it becomes at a Texas Hold 'Em table. Troll dolls, lucky hats, and special motions with their hands may give a player the luck they are seeking.

Whatever their method, just go with it and do not try to ask them to defend their decision. Texas Hold 'Em should be fun, and people should be free to use whatever methods they feel gives them the advantage.

Sure it might be fun to question why if their lucky charm is so lucky to have them lose 5 games in a row, but it is simply bad table manners.

Although, it sounds like a strategy to throw someone off their game, right? Don't do it.

Don't Be a Commentator

Admittedly, I have done this when playing with friends in a joking matter. I lean over with a grin and a raised eyebrow and say something like, "Do they have the straight or are they just holding a pair?" I gave them a hard time as they debated raising or folding.

Amongst friends, and those not sensitive about losing a few bucks while playing cards, eating pizza and drinking a few beers, this is okay.

Don't do it at a table.

Do not be a commentator whether you are playing or have folded.

You never know what information you are going to let out. If there are three hearts in the Flop and a player raises, do not say something like, "Oh, could it be a flush in the works?" Because whether you are playing or not, you could give away someone's hand or make other players question the intent. You could lose a game for someone or wipe away a strategy.

Don't Be a Sore Winner, or a Sore Lose, or an Instigator

Imagine you just played out a hand and lost.

"Nice work. Feel free to keep handing me your money."

Is that what you want to hear? Some people love being competitive to the point they are jerks whether they win, lose or are playing. Do what is in your best interest, not someone else's. And don't goad someone into betting.

"You think you got me beat?"

"Come on, it's $10 more. Don't wuss out now."

Do you really want to be the guy who makes everyone have a bad time and walk away from a table?

You aren't razzing friends. These are people with money who are playing to win. It's much different than poker night with a group of friends where the money makes things interesting.

The Showdown

Never insist that someone shows their hand. If you have to show your hand based on the way the cards were dealt, and you won, just accept the fact that you won and do not insist the other players show their cards. If you are out and you want to know what the other players had, again, do not try to get them to show them to you.

Aside from these few things, there is very little you can do at a Texas Hold 'Em table that is a 'never, ever.' You can ask questions about betting, or the cards, or the way to play, and you will probably get answers. You will obviously be seen as a beginner though and the more seasoned sharks will smell the blood.

Chapter 7
Witnessing the Impossible

Back when there was a hotel and casino in Las Vegas called the Imperial Palace, they had turned a portion of one of their floors into a Texas Hold 'Em room. Gambling at the Imperial Palace was considerably less expensive than at casinos such as the Bellagio or Paris and I was a young man interested in testing his luck at the poker tables.

It was daytime in Vegas and the room was not very busy. I went in on my own and found a table that was a little more than half filled. I did not even plan on gambling much money and it was a low stakes table. As a beginner, I was playing very conservatively, feeling out the table and trying my best to play with a poker face.

I do not remember what I had. I very well may not have folded right off the bat but there were a few players who remained into the Flop, then a couple folded into the Turn.

Finally, the River…and two players remained.

The five community cards were as followed:

4, 4, Ace (Heart), King (Heart), Jack (Heart).

These two players were betting all they could against one another until one finally caved and said, "Check."

It was on the other to reveal their cards.

"I don't know what you have…" he started and then threw down his hole cards.

He had the Queen of Hearts and the 10 of Hearts.

The man got a Royal Straight Flush. The probability of getting such a hand is 0.003%. Out of every combination in poker, all 2,598,960 combinations, there are only four ways to get this hand.

The table erupted in shock and surprise.

Then the other player revealed his cards.

He was holding the other two fours.

He had a four of a kind! A probability of 0.2% and only 13 ways to achieve this hand.

Again, the table lost it and filled the room with cheers, gasps, and laughter of witnessing the near impossible two hands.

The manager of the department even came over to investigate the noise and congratulate the players.

It was an exciting thing to behold and something I always think about before sitting down at a table.

There are many lessons in poker that can relate to this story.

Lesson #1:

One lesson learned is that anything can happen in poker and even the sure thing can almost always be beaten. Who would have thought that a four of a kind could actually lose?

There is a quote from an episode of Star Trek: The Next Generation that Captain Jean-Luc Picard (played by Patrick

Stewart) tells to Lt. Commander Data (played by Brent Spiner) I feel sums up this scenario:

"It is possible to make no mistakes and still lose. That is not a weakness. That is life."

Lesson #2:

The guy who won had a curious smile when he placed his two cards face up. He was excited to present his cards, but there was literally no way for him to lose.

The losing player stoically showed his cards and kept his poker face, accepting his loss and ready to play another round.

Both acted appropriately and were good sports. There is nothing skillful about the way the cards are dealt but rather how the game is played. Both accepted the outcome.

Accept how the cards are dealt, whether or not they are in your favor.

Lesson #3:

Every new hand can be a winner or a loser. But each new hand is an opportunity. The man who lost continued to play, as did the winner. Neither won the next hand.

I hope in your playing you get to see an amazing showdown like the one I witnessed. It gives you an appreciation of the game, an unbelievable level of excitement and shows how possible the impossible can be.

It also gives you one hell of a story to tell, and one you would not soon forget.

Chapter 8
Your First Time

Perhaps the best way to acquaint yourself with Texas Hold 'Em is to play poker. If you are heading to a casino and you are itching to test your luck and skills at Texas Hold 'Em, but you are not quite sure you have the knowledge, pump a few dollars into the poker machines. There are plenty to choose from and most will probably cost you a quarter per game.

What playing on a machine will do is show you the frequency in which you can expect a winning hand. While most poker machines will have various five card poker games, you can still see how frequently the major winning hands will come up. Sure, it is nice to double your quarter into 50 cents with two pair or even triple it to 75 cents with a three of a kind but what is the likelihood that high hands will come your way?

It is nice to win on the poker machines, but most of the time you will probably lose your money; hey, that's what they are designed to do. But take the experience and put it to good use.

One tactic is to look at the first 2 cards dealt on a poker machine. They all come up at the same time so it might take some handiwork. Literally. Put your hand over the area where three of the five cards pop up. Based on the two visible cards (your "hole cards"), how would you bet? Or would you fold it away?

Let's say your first two cards are a 6 and an 8, same suit. Not bad, but not very good and probability-wise not very promising.

What would you do? Then you can move your hand and pretend you have the Flop. Would you have been wise to bet?

On the poker machines, you can replace as many cards as you want. If you don't mind risking a few quarters, take two of the cards (not the two you didn't cover up, remember, those are your "hole cards") and replace them. Now you have a set of seven cards. What was the best 5 card hand you could create?

I believe that by betting money, you will learn quicker but learning poker on the machines is a very cheap option too.

A super cheap option is to just grab a deck of cards, sit at your kitchen table and deal like you were playing. Shuffle the deck and deal yourself two hole cards. Think about how you would bet and then continue with the Flop, the Turn, then the River. Of course, this tactic works well if you can get a friend interested in playing a few hands so you can see how you may decide to continue based on another player raising the bet.

Bad Vibes

Ya know, you probably are not going to get great vibes when you sit down at the table. This is not like every other game in the casino – your goal is to take these people's money, not a casino's money.

Keep that in mind. Being friendly and talkative is not necessarily a bad thing, but sometimes people want to play with their best poker face and the cards close to their vest.

They may also think you are looking for their tells.

Have Fun

Don't bet more than you can afford and don't forget to have fun. As a beginner, you can only be so serious.

Play with Friends

If you want to get a feel for the game before going to the casino, try getting a small game together at your house.

I can relate this advice to playing Blackjack with friends. There were only three of us, and I played the dealer. One of my friends could not get a good set of cards to save his life while the other was doing fairly well. If you play with friends, you can see how the hole cards play out once the Flop, Turn, and River are dealt. You can see how others play and the likelihood of getting those high combinations and how frequently you can squeeze together a pair.

The New Fish

If you can't spot the fish at the table, you are the fish.

Fish is a term used for a poker player who is not very good or looks as if they are making it a point to lose all their money.

Developing skills in Texas Hold 'Em is just like trying to advance your knowledge in just about anything else – it will take some time. While you may not lose or have the personality to play erratically, you are still new so don't go in with the expectation that you are going to walk away with an envious amount of chips.

As you continue playing, you will begin to see how the newer players act and do not have the same skillset as you do.

While it is hard to determine, if you want to have fun, you probably need to be playing against people at the same skill level as you. One suggestion is to play low stakes. The expert players will less likely be the ones trying to take the small pots from the nervous, new players.

Poker is an exciting game and playing Texas Hold 'Em at the casino is a riveting way to spend some time. If you have the basic knowledge and you are willing to take a chance, you have the opportunity enjoy some winning hands.

Now, go out there and have some fun.

Blackjack:

How to Play Blackjack

A Beginner to Expert Guide to Get You from the Sidelines to Running the Craps Table, Reduce Your Risk, and Have Fun

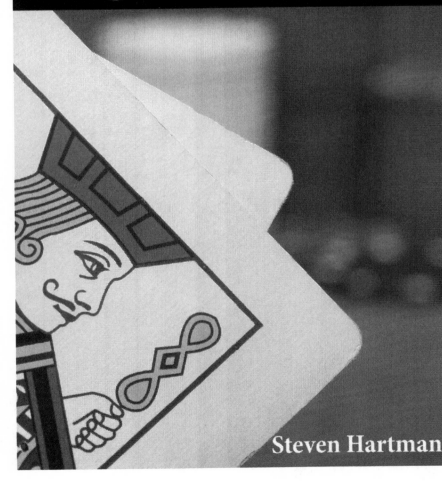

HOW TO PLAY BLACKJACK

a beginner to expert guide

Steven Hartman

Table of Contents

Chapter 1
Welcome to the Blackjack Table!

After pumping dollars into the slot machine and staring at a screen, you get up and notice the table games section of the casino. Brightly lit from can lights shining downward and the crisp green felt of the line of games making you think of the cash in your wallet or purse?

There is a row of blackjack tables. Some have a dealer standing with their hands clasped idly in front of them or pressed along the cushion running along the felt. They stare at the gamblers roaming the casino eagerly awaiting the next person to place a chip and test their luck. Other tables are crammed with players, the people behind them shifting to look over their shoulder, and you hear the loud clasp of a hand and the cheer of the table, "Blackjack!"

Some tables are hot, some are just warming up, and some are presided over by a cruel dealer who seems to have the luck that any player would crave.

The truth is it is all in the cards' each one shuffled meticulously by man or machine and dealt out randomly. The dealer has the same luck you do.

That's the fun of it though.

Blackjack is a level playing field, yet a collaborative field where it's the players vs. the dealer. Each strategic move, combined with the luck of the draw, inches the odds of the house taking your money down more and more until it is near even.

- The odds of winning any single hand of Blackjack are approximately 42%

- The odds of tying with the dealer and not winning or losing is approximately 8%

- The odds of losing a hand of Blackjack is 50%

Blackjack is combination of your skill, the skill of the other players at the table, and using the cards to your advantage to eke out a win.

What This Book Will Teach You

The Absolute Basics

The first part of this book is going to explain the bare bones of Blackjack. This will be a short introduction into what it takes to win at Blackjack and the value of the cards. This section will also explain the Blackjack table itself.

Playing the Game

We will then explain the game in further detail and teach you how to play the game of Blackjack as well as what to expect even before the cards are being dealt and when you win, lose or push.

Beyond the Basics

Now that you know the table and the basics, it's time to go beyond the basics. What are some extra bets you can make? How does your decision to play affect the entire table? And the best practices that give you a higher chance at success?

Never, Ever!

There is proper etiquette when at the Blackjack table including rules from the casino. I will also share some ways not to not upset friends who may be watching. We will go over some of the "Never, Ever" scenarios so you can feel confident when sitting down.Page Break

Moneymaking Tips

We all want to walk away from the Blackjack table with more money than when we arrived. While I can't guarantee you always will, I have found two methods that have helped me make some money while playing Blackjack. I will share those methods with you in this section.

Your First Time

Finally, we will give you a few tips on what you should do when you sit down at the table for the first time.

Blackjack is a thrilling, fast paced game yet not intimidating once you sit down making diving into the table games section of the casino easy.

Are you ready to learn Blackjack?

Chapter 2
The Absolute Basics

At the basic level, Blackjack is a fairly simple game. It involves a player trying to exceed the dealer's hand, preferably getting to 21 without going over.

By accumulating cards with numerical values, the closer you are to 21 the greater the chance of winning.

If you exceed 21, you lose, or what is called "bust".

Blackjack is played with a standard deck of cards, minus the jokers, and each card number represents a number between 1 and 11. Most casinos will use six decks at the Blackjack and they are generally dealt through a device called a "shoe".

The suits do not matter in the basic game of Blackjack.

Here is breakdown of the cards:

- A (Aces) = 1 or 11

- 2 = 2

- 3 = 3

- 4 = 4

- 5 = 5

- 6 = 6

- 7 = 7

- 8 = 8

- 9 = 9

- 10 = 10

- J (Jack) = 10

- Q (Queen) = 10

- K (King) = 10

    Pretty easy to remember, right?

***

The Blackjack table is fairly simple as well.

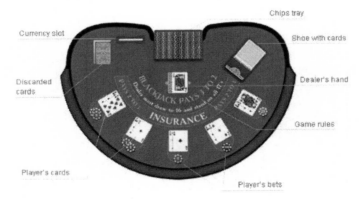

There are circles indicating where each player places their chips, a line explaining insurance, what a Blackjack pays and the dealer's rules.

Bets are placed in the circles and cards are dealt right above it.

The shoe, where the cards are dealt, will either be on the side of the table or fed from a machine right at the edge of the table.

If it is a shoe, the dealer will discard the used cards on the opposite side of the table. Once the table has filtered through a certain number of cards, the dealer reshuffles all of the cards. Sometimes the Blackjack tables will have two series' of six decks, two different colors to distinguish there are two different sets, in which case, while one is being dealt the other is being automatically shuffled in a machine.

If the dealer does have to reshuffle the multiple decks on their own, they will have what is called a cut card. The cut card is a plastic, brightly colored card that the dealer gives to a player to cut the deck. Once the deck is cut, the plastic card is placed toward the end of the deck and used as a marker to indicate when enough cards have been played and it is time to shuffle the deck.

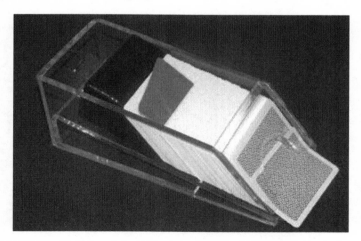

Superstition will sometimes be a factor and players will opt-out of cutting the deck. Also, if you have ever been the one to cut the deck and the table is not very hot, you may feel the urge to decline cutting the next time. Bad cuts happen.

On the flipside, if there is a player who had a really good cut, the table generally wants them to cut the deck again.

The only time you really can't refuse to cut is if you are the only one at the table.

If cards are dealt via machine, the dealer will most likely return the cards back to the machine where it automatically shuffles.

Now that you know the meaning of the cards and what to expect at a basic Blackjack table, let's learn how to play the game!

Chapter 3
Playing the Game

To learn how to start playing Blackjack, we are going to pretend that the only two players at the Blackjack table are you and the dealer.

The dealer will deal you a card face up, and then deal them self a card face up (called, conveniently, the up card). Then they will deal you a second card face up, and then deal them self a card face down (called the hole card).

Everyone sees your cards and the players are only allowed to see the dealer's one card.

Now you basically have two choices:

- Hit – Get another card

- Stand – Stay with what you were dealt with

You can say "Hit" but the eyes in the sky generally want visual proof so to signal you want to hit, you can tap your hand next to your cards.

If you want to stay, you wave your hand over your card like you were doing a horizontal karate chop, although not as quickly.

The dealer has a certain set of rules provided by the house on hitting and staying and the player can pretty much play the game however they choose.

Dealer Rules:

Rules may differ from casinos and locations but these are the basics:

- A dealer must hit to 17

- If the dealer's cards equal 2 to 16, they must hit

- If the dealer's cards equal 17 to 21, they must stand

You are not subject to these rules. You can essentially stand with two Aces, although no one in the world would advise this.

Based on these rules, the player can strategize whether hitting or standing can help them win the hand.

Once you decide to finally stand, the dealer flips his card over and hits to 17 or stays with the two cards they have been dealt.

There are now three outcomes:

- You win

- You lose

- You push

A win means you receive a payout equal to your bet - $10 bet equals a $10 win. You win by either having a higher sum of your cards than the dealer without busting or the dealer busts. The best way to win though is to have a Blackjack which is the one way that you win automatically - the dealer deals you 21 or Blackjack! This would be an Ace and any card equal to 10 (10, Jack, Queen, King). You get paid immediately your hand is over.

When you win, the dealer will keep your cards and your money on the table until all the hands conclude in which they will pay you and then pull the cards away.

To lose means you grunt below your breath and curse that the cards did not land how you would have wished. It also means you lose your money. You can lose if a dealer has a Blackjack, they have a higher sum of their cards than you, or you busted.

When you lose, the dealer immediately takes your money and the cards away.

A push means you and the dealer tied and you keep your money.

Once all the hands are cleared, the dealer will wait for the bets to be placed and start the next deal.

Simple as that! It will only take you a few hands to get the idea of how Blackjack is played. If you have money at stake, you are more likely going to learn quicker.

Now that you understand how the game of Blackjack is played, it's time to go beyond the basics.

Chapter 4
Beyond the Basics

Everyone plays the game how they want to. What I will explain are the general rules that most of the "intelligent" play by. When you play based on these rules, you minimize the chances that you will lose considerably and increase your odds of winning or pushing to near 50%.

But this is gambling and the casino always ensures it has the edge. The good news is that in Blackjack they have a very small edge too so playing based on the following strategy helps you get closer to winning.

You sit down at the Blackjack table and the dealer deals you a 4 and a Jack (equal to 10) for a total of 14. Their up card is a 10. They will check to see if their hole card is an Ace. For the sake of this explanation, it is not so the dealer looks to you to see what you want to do.

So, what do you do? Do you hit? Do you stay?

Remember, the goal is to win by having a higher number than the dealer or having the dealer bust. You know that the dealer must hit to 17.

Depending on what the dealer is showing determines the next step. The chances of any card being a 10 are 4:13 or approximately 30%.

That being the case, if you hit on your 14, and the dealer deals an 8, 9, 10, Jack, Queen or King, you lose immediately. Not only is your chance of getting a card equivalent to ten 30%, you also have an approximately 15% chance of getting an 8 or a 9 card too!

The odds seem pretty lousy, right?

The chances of you getting a bust card (the card that makes a player/dealer exceed 21) look really good, don't they?

Well, the best strategy is to actually hit.

Why?

Just as the likelihood of you busting, there is a higher likelihood that the dealer has a 7, 8, 9, 10, Jack, Queen or King which means they have a better chance of beating you if you do nothing. Just the odds of the dealer having another 10 card are almost at 30%.

When in doubt, play like the dealer. Remember, casinos want to make money. There's a reason they hit up to 17 and stay on anything above.

So, hit and hope for the best.

Hope for the best? Yes. It's gambling so whether the Roulette wheel is spinning or the dice are being rolled or you are press a button on the slot machine; that is what you hope for.

This is just one scenario out of hundreds that can play out but I wanted to use it as an example of how the frequency of tens can affect the outcome.

So here is the most basic and best strategy to abide by:

- If the dealer is showing any number between 2 and 6 then you hit until you have 12.

- If the dealer is showing any number between 7 and the Ace, you hit until you have at least 17.

Blackjack

A Blackjack is when you get 21 from the first two cards you are dealt. One card will be an Ace and one card will be a Ten, Jack, Queen or King.

A Blackjack pays 3:2 which means if you bet $10 and you get Blackjack, you will be paid $15. If you are playing at a low stakes table or playing at a single deck table, the casino will sometimes pay 6:5 for a Blackjack. Your $10 bet will therefore pay $12 if you get a Blackjack.

A Blackjack is an automatic win and you will get paid immediately.

There is one instance in which you won't get paid though; if the dealer has a Blackjack too. If the dealer is showing an Ace and you have a Blackjack, they will ask if you want even money before they see what their face down card is.

If you can't lose, why would you do this?

Because if the dealer also has a Blackjack you would push (in a few instances, the a dealer's Blackjack is a loss for everyone) – no money won, no money lost.

There is no right or wrong way to play this but most players would prefer to go down fighting than accept even money.

*Blackjack Superstition: If a dealer deals out an Ace, you'll notice that the player who receives the card as well as some of the others, and even sometimes the dealer, will tap or knock on the edge of the table or the felt twice. This is a superstitious move in hopes that a ten will show up to accommodate that Ace.

Insurance

When you look at the Blackjack table, you see a line that says Insurance. This is an option when the dealer shows an Ace as their up card and may have a Blackjack.

Prior to looking at the hole card, the dealer will ask if anyone wants insurance.

This is a side bet between you and the dealer. Insurance odds are 2:1 and you receive a payout only if the dealer has a Blackjack. If you bet $10 for insurance and the dealer has Blackjack, you will win $20 but you do lose your initial bet.

If you have a Blackjack and the dealer shows an Ace, offering you even money is also considered a form of insurance.

I have been playing Blackjack for 15 years and I have seen someone say yes to insurance once; they lost.

Splitting

If you are dealt two cards of the same value, you can split them by placing a second bet equal to your first one down. An initial $10 bet means you will need to put another $10 and split your cards

After your cards get split, then it is like you are playing two completely separate hands.

Why would you want to split your cards? Generally the two sets of cards that are "must" splits are 8-8 and A-A because everything revolves around trying to get those tens. What's better? 8-8 equaling 16? Or the opportunity to have two sets of 18?

Same with the Aces. How does two sets of 21 sound as oppose to hitting on a sum of 2 or 12? Even if you received 9's that gives you 20 and a good chance at winning your money.

Here's the kicker with 21. If you split Aces and get your tens, you don't get a Blackjack and won't get immediately paid. The good news is you won't lose; but, if the dealer is able to hit to 21, you will push.

Of course that is not guaranteed but you can see how having that 30% chance of landing a ten card makes splitting seem like a wise investment.

Hypothetically, let's say you split a pair of eights and one of those gets another eight. You are allowed to split again.

Double Down

Another way to make some extra money on a hand is to double down. You most frequently see this when a player has been dealt a hand equaling 10 or 11.

Let's say you get dealt a 6 and a 5. Wouldn't it be nice to double your bet and get that 10? This is the idea behind doubling down and getting a 10 is the outcome people are betting on.

When you double down, you are matching your bet in order to receive 1 additional card.

Again, when you double down, you only get 1 single card so if the dealer deals you a 2 and not a 10 then that means your cards have a total value of 13 which significantly decreases your odds of winning against the dealer.

This is what gambling is all about though.

Sometimes people are not feeling quite as lucky but still want to increase their bet for a chance to make more money if they win. You can call "Double for less" and place a smaller bet alongside your original bet and get 1 additional card.

- Double Down with a $10 bet means you place $10 next to your original bet

- Double for Less with a $10 bet means you place a denomination less than $10 next to your original bet (ex: $5 chip next to your initial $10 bet).

Surrender

Rare is it that you will see someone surrender but this option is available at many casinos and allows you to surrender your hand if you feel you are going to lose.

This option is only allowed before you decide to hit, stand, double down, etc. It is the one and only decision you can make after your initial cards are dealt.

When you surrender, the casino takes half your bet and you keep half. Players view this as an option if they feel they are going to lose and want to save a little money. A good example would be if a player has 16 and the dealer is showing a card equivalent to ten.

Additional Bets

There are many additional bets that may be available at your Blackjack table. Unfortunately, many consider them sucker bets and, to be truthful, they are not too far off. Casinos always want to make money and will do everything they can to squeeze an additional dollar out of their customers.

Nonetheless, the additional bets are fun to do and it certainly is not impossible to win. Winning or losing on these additional bets does not affect the final outcome of the actual Blackjack hand, that includes if the dealer has a Blackjack; you can win an additional bet and actually lose the hand.

Here are some of the common versions you will find at casino tables. While the cost for placing a bet may vary, for the sake of the examples, we will assume they are just a buck.

- Perfect Pairs

- Although it may go by many versions, when you bet on a Perfect Pair, you are placing a $1 bet that your first two cards will be two Kings or two Jacks, etc. There may be a higher payout if the pairs are the same suit.

- Ex: 2 x Queen of Hearts

- Lady Luck

- This additional bet plays off the Queen as being the alluring detail of the action. Getting two queens, a queen and king, two queens of the same suit, or a variety of other versions that you could conceivably get on initial deal will pay a certain amount for each $1 bet.

- "21 + 3"

- For "21 + 3", this is similar to a three card poker hand. Using the two cards dealt to you plus the dealer's face card, the idea is to make a poker hand that pays out. Three of a kind, flushes and straights are the likeliest payouts.

Not always an additional bet, but sometimes casinos will offer a higher payout if you hit three times for a total of five cards and you reach 21; also known as a Five Card Charlie. There are some casinos that pay 2:1 for achieving this feat.

If your Blackjack table offers one of these additional bets, there will be an additional circle outside of your betting circle where you can place it. There will also be a list of payouts and how to play. If you have any questions regarding how to play, the dealer will be able to guide you in the right direction.

Speaking of the dealers...

Tipping your Dealer

While a dealer will be happy to take a tip at any point during your tenure at the Blackjack table, you are also able to place a bet on their behalf. Why tip $1 when you can turn it into a $2 bet.

Simply place however much you want to tip the dealer in front of your bet. Most dealers will recognize what you are doing.

The hand plays as normal and if you win, they win. If you lose, though, they don't get a tip.

While the dealer does not have an outcome in how the cards fall, they will be grateful for the gesture. Once the hand is played, the dealer takes the money away. Even if they win, they cannot "let it ride" and play again.

If you place a bet for a dealer and you decide to double down on your bet, guess what, you have to place an additional chip down for them as well.

Playing With Others

So far we have been providing examples with just the one player and the dealer. But this game is often played with more players around the table and how the cards play out is often based on the choices that are made.

While most "mistakes" are made by the newer players or drunk players who want to test their luck, when money is involved, many people have opinions and if other players divert to strategies they don't believe in then it often garners a shaking of the head and a murmur under the breath.

The truth is that no one knows what card is going to come up next so what seems like a silly move may save the table while another may spell doom. All people have are the odds but no one knows what the dealer's hole card is or the next card to come out of the shoe.

The player sitting to the left of the dealer is considered first base and they can set the tone for the table. Their decisions on how to play directly impacts the rest of the table. If they hit one card too many then, for example, the ten that the next player wants or doesn't want may appear.

First base is the one who receives the option to hit, stand, etc., first and the dealer continues around the table after the respective player officially stands.

The player who is sitting to the right of the dealer, also the last person at a full table who has a chance to hit before the dealer goes, is called third base. The third base seat is also critical to playing a strategic game of Blackjack. One of the challenges is when the dealer shows a five or six but the player has cards equaling 11 or less. Sure it may seem like the right move to hit but if that player gets their ten, they could get blamed for taking the dealer's bust card if the dealer pulls out a win.

If it matters to you what the other players think then it would be wise to play with the strategy set forth in this book. Speaking of which...

Cheat Sheets

Imagine being able to have the ideal strategy at your fingertips. Wouldn't it be nice to know if you should hit, stay or split on any number of possibilities?

You can.

Most casinos allow players to have a cheat sheet right in front of them, so long as it is not on your phone or any electronic device. They even sell them in the gift shop!

Why would a casino allow you to use this?

Because even with all the right answers in the palm of your hands the house still holds the favorable odds. In fact, the house holds a statistical edge over the players by approximately 8%. When players play consistently by the best strategy, these odds drop to below 1%. That is still enough money to comp drinks and keep the lights on.

Additional bets and bad choices are also what help the casino stay in business.

What the casino frowns upon is counting cards. There is nothing wrong with suspecting that the next card is going to be equivalent to a ten or a number card but the art of counting cards is grounds for removal, usually for good and at every casino.

Most likely you will not run into this problem for several reasons:

- If you are reading a book on how to play Blackjack, it's a good chance that you haven't discovered your ability to count cards.

- Casinos use either a machine to reshuffle used cards into a deck or shuffle up to six decks (a total of 312 cards) for use at one time. This makes it extremely difficult to actually count cards; but still that's 104 cards that equal 10.

There are Blackjack tables that use single decks or double decks though and this is where counting cards gives an advantage to winning. But as long as you don't practice beyond how many tens may have shown up in the last few hands, you have nothing to worry about.

Now that you know how to play and a few strategies to get you going, let's talk about the things you should never do at a Blackjack table.

Chapter 5
Never, Ever

With any table at the casino there are a few rules that you must abide by in order to remain at the table and to keep the others happy.

Casino

First off, never touch the cards. Even if the hand is over and you lost, do not touch those cards. Only the dealer is allowed to deal, place and remove the cards on the table.

That being said, there are always exceptions to the rules. There are a few casinos out there that offer a version of Blackjack that gets dealt with the cards face down and you can pick them up. This is generally a one or two deck version of Blackjack and the gimmick being that you get to hold on to the cards but makes it impossible for the other players at the table to see what lays before them. In this version, when you stand, you place your cards face down under your chips.

Speaking of chips...

Once you put your chips down, you can't touch those either. The reason being is you can sneak a chip on or off if you feel you are going to win or lose, respectively.

When you double down or split, you tell the dealer by placing the chips beside your set of chips, never on top. The dealer will usually be able to tell what you want to do as the likelihood of someone doubling down on 2 x eights or a pair of Aces is a strange concept will warrant a call to the pit boss so they have a witness of what the player wants to do.

Don't stack your chips though. Side-by-side is the right way.

When you approach the Blackjack table and you pull out your money, make sure to wait until the current round is complete. You do not want to mess up any cards or give the dealer a hard time. Plus, they are not going to give you chips at that moment anyway because they are currently dealing a hand.

When you place your money down, put it next to the circle where the chips go or in front. If you place it in the circle, they may figure you are betting it. Now, if you are laying out $100 in twenties, you would think they would obviously know what is going on. Yes, they should know but you shouldn't assume so.

Let's say you put a twenty down at a $5 table or $10 table; you can now see how a twenty dollar bill could look like a bet.

I've done this before and once the dealer starts dealing, the bet is set. I honestly can't remember if I won my $20 back but I certainly remembered to follow this rule from that point on.

The next casino-related never, ever has to do with etiquette and sitting at the table.

- Your phone – You can't put your phone on the table, hold it in your hand or answer it. This means if your friend is calling or texting you wondering where you are, you have to step away from the table to answer. If it is in the middle of the hand, do not walk away. Finish your hand and then call/text your friend back. They will hold your spot.

- Your drink – Whether it's a water or an alcoholic drink you're enjoying at the table, don't put your drink down on the felt of the table. The dealer should be able to provide you with a beverage holder. The last thing you want to do is spill your drink on the table or leave a condensation ring. Not only does a spilled drink stall everything and often empty the table, it can also ruin the cards.

- Your cigarette – Keep cigarettes in the ashtray, unless you are smoking it, of course. If you like having it in your hand, keep the cigarette below the table. This is a courtesy to the other players and the dealer who may not want smoke in their face; it also prevents ash from landing on the table or accidentally burning a hole into the felt.

Friends

During the peak times at casinos, a Blackjack table may be crowded and you may find yourself standing behind a friend who is a little down on their luck. Although it may be enticing to sit down in their place when they decide to call it quits, I would advise against this.

The reason is simple: jealousy.

Let's say that you suddenly hit a winning streak. How would that make your friend feel? For the sake of maintaining friendships, I would recommend not sitting down in a seat a friend has occupied.

If the situation is reversed and you are the one who isn't getting the good cards and your friend wants to take over the seat, this is when I would recommend you walk away and find another table.

In the end, the cards all land differently. Just because the next person to take over a seat is winning doesn't mean it was going to play out that way. The dealer could shuffle differently or dump a card because there is a new player sitting down or a pause in the game (a common occurrence).

Of course, playing at the same table with friends is fun so long as everyone's luck is running the same way.

Page BreakQuick Story

One time I was sitting in an apartment with two friends and we decided to play Blackjack with some poker chips. I was the dealer and one of my friends won more than they were losing but the other friend could not get a win to save his life. Although there was no money in play, he was increasingly getting frustrated.

Imagine being at a Blackjack table and this is happening. Over matters of money, avoid giving your friend a hard time and don't be surprised if they walk away.

Players

Everyone plays their own way and, yes, sometimes someone's decision can negatively affect the entire table. Sometimes luck pays off and you pull two tens when splitting nines (not advised) and sometimes you double down on 9 and the dealer gives you 2, then the player next to you hits his 16 and gets a ten card. While it is your money and you have every right to play how you choose, I would bear in mind that it is other people's money too and I recommend a level of courtesy.

Basic strategy is generally the best way to keep your chances of winning high.

Bet More Than You Intend to Lose

You would think that this makes all the sense in the world and that you would abide by it but sometimes you get lost in your desire to make the money back. Perhaps it started out as a winning streak that went cold and you felt that, if you keep at it, your luck will turn.

It might. It might not.

Blackjack isn't like the stock market though that has a history of giving a return in the long run.

There are times you might do incredibly well at one table only to find your chips are depleting quickly at another.

Winning is fun and chasing that win is exciting but it isn't worth losing more than you can afford to lose. You may have just sat down at a Blackjack table and pull out $20 and, Boom!, you lose it right away. So you dig in for more money and within a few hands it's gone. You've been at the table for 5 minutes and not only did you lose $40 but you also didn't really have any fun. It's hard to suck up your pride and leave but you should know when it's time to cut your losses and walk away.

Quick Story

I wish I listened to this advice several years ago when I was in Las Vegas. I was enjoying one of the smaller, cheaper casinos that are on the strip. At the time, they famously had a $3 Blackjack table and the place was fairly empty which was unusual, the place is generally packed. I sat down at the table and started gambling away. I knew I should have walked away but I kept pouring more and more money into the table hoping I would get it back. Eventually, I lost $75 playing $3 Blackjack. Considering I did win a little here and there, we are still looking at losing a minimum of 25 times!

You've got to know when to hold 'em / Know when to fold 'em / Know when to walk away / And know when to run

~ Kenny Rogers, The Gambler

Chapter 6
Moneymaking Tips

I can't promise that you will make money when gambling; Las Vegas was built on people losing money. What I can offer you is a few tips that I have used and others have used that have helped them walk away from the table with money in their pocket.

Each tip is given on the assumption that you are doing pretty decently at the Blackjack table.

Tip #1: Pocket your winnings

Say you have been sitting at the table for twenty minutes or so and you look down and see a collection of chips in front of you. You have obviously been winning more than losing and you want to walk away from the table with proof that you had a successful run. Every so often, take a chip and shove it in your pocket. You will notice that it will become a habit.

Now, you would love to collect a stack of chips, your accumulated winnings, and walk away when things start to get a little cold.

Most likely, players play until they are out of money, and you probably will too because you think anything you lost you can make it back

Stashing chips in your pocket and telling yourself that when you are out you are leaving is a good way to exit the table with money.

I have done this quite a few times with success. I wasn't a high roller or anything. I would sit down at a Blackjack table with

$20 or $40 and start playing. If my funds ran out and I have been pocketing, I've strolled out of there with $100.

Another tip to add on to this is, if you are at a $10 table and you are collecting $5 chips, once you get a decent amount, ask the dealer to color out a few of them. This means they will take your $5 chips and upgrade them into $25 chips. Pocket that. It's much harder to toss a $25 or even $50 chip to play than it is two $5 chips.

Quick Story

There is a down side to pocketing chips – not finding all of them. There were times I met my family in Las Vegas and my sister would do this method and shove chips into her purse as she was winning. Well, it was pretty standard that I would get a call or text after we all parted ways and went home that stated she found a chip or two once she emptied out her purse.

Now, I was living in Los Angeles and she was living on the east coast. I was more likely to make it to Vegas much sooner than she was so she would end up mailing it to me with my birthday present several months later or give it to me when we saw each other again at Thanksgiving.

Remember to check your pockets and/or your purse thoroughly if you are pocketing chips.

Tip #2: Add a chip on each win

I have made some pretty good money quickly with this method and, the good news is, you only have to win a few times in a row for it to really start paying off.

We are assuming you sat down at a $10 Blackjack table. You bet two $5 chips and you win. Naturally, the dealer gives you two more $5 chips.

Take one of those $5 chips and add it to your bet.

Every time you win, you keep adding 1 chip. Here's how quickly it can add up:

- 1st bet = $10

- Win $10, keep $5, place additional $5

- 2nd bet = $15

- Win $15, keep $10, place additional $5

- 3rd bet = $20

- Win $20, keep $15, place additional $5

- 4th bet = $25

- Win $25, keep $20, place additional $5

If you win that 4th bet, you are now up $70 from your original $10 bet just by adding $5 for every win.

If you win four times in a row, you are starting to win considerably more than if you just kept betting $10 per hand.

The tricky part with this is doubling down and splitting.

If you get two Aces and you have a $25 bet, you must match it with another $25 giving you the real possibility of losing $50 in a single hand.

Doubling down is not as threatening if you're nervous. Remember, you can double for less. So, even though you have a $25 bet, you can double for $10.

This method has worked out well for me when it starts to pay off. I have had friends and family who will do this as well with varying degrees of success.

Of course, I then have a friend come over to the table I'm at and their eyes bug out when they see I'm betting $45 on a single hand.

Here's the trick. If you lose a hand, start over. It may seem strange betting $40 on one hand only to bet $10 on the next but that seems to be the best method.

Quick Story

I used this method quite successfully once and had a great winning streak. I made it to the point that I ended up losing on a $55 bet but that was after I made over $300 on less than 10 hands of Blackjack thanks to a few Blackjacks being dealt and a double down opportunity. This is after I started out with just $10.

The flip side of that coin is putting down $20 and losing two hands in a row. Sometimes the cards don't always land in your favor.

Bonus tip: Play by the rules

Sure it's a silly tip to consistently hit on again and again but it really does give you the best odds at winning.

Chapter 7
Your First Time

When you are first starting out, take things slow. The dealer is often a good resource for helping you along as far as what your options are and how things are playing out. They will often shy away from telling you whether you would hit or stand simply pointing out they are obligated to hit until they are over 16 and stay on 17 and above.

You can even make a quick stop at the gift shop to pick up the cheat sheet and reference it until you get the hang of things.

Find a low stakes table and place down the minimum for each hand. You will soon learn how to play Blackjack and enjoy seeking out the tables whenever you are at a casino.

And don't forget, when you are dealt that Ace, tap the table twice and watch for the face card.

Blackjack!

Thank You!

I hope you enjoyed this book as much as I've enjoyed writing it! If you would please take 20 seconds of your time to review this book, it would mean so much to me, to hear how you've enjoyed it.

Leave A Review here

http://bit.ly/UGGuide

53318345R00080

Made in the USA
Middletown, DE
26 November 2017